THOUGHT SYMBOLS MAGICK GUIDE BOOK

Manifest Your Desires in Life using the Secret Power of Sigil Magic and Thought Forms

©2015 Colin G Smith

www.AwesomeMindSecrets.com

Disclaimer

This eBook is for educational purposes only, and is not intended to be a substitute for professional counselling, therapy or medical treatment. Nothing in this eBook is intended to diagnose or treat any pathology or diseased condition of the mind or body. The author will not be held responsible for any results of reading or applying the information.

Table of Contents

About Colin G Smith:

For over ten years Colin G Smith has been driven to find the very best methods for creating effective personal change. He is a NLP Master Practitioner, writer & author who has written several books including, *"The NLP ToolBox: Your Guide Book to Neuro Linguistic Programming NLP Techniques"* and, *"Creative Problem Solving Techniques To Change Your Life."*

Visit his Amazon Author Page here:

http://www.Amazon.com/author/colingsmith

What are Thought Symbols and Sigil Magick?

Thought Symbols is a term synonymous with *Sigil Magick*. The term sigil derives from the Latin sigillum, meaning *"seal"*, though it may also be related to the Hebrew, *"segula,"* meaning *"word, action, or item of spiritual effect, talisman."* The use of the term today is derived from Renaissance magic, which was inspired by the magical traditions of antiquity.

Sigil Magick enables us to manifest our desires into reality by transforming our conscious desires into a graphical device (*Thought Symbol*) which allows us to by-pass the sabotaging ego-mind and instead tap right into our sub-conscious resources and greater universal powers.

- We're manifesting our reality all the time with our thoughts

- Our thoughts can be very powerful

- The conscious ego mind is very limited in comparison to the vast sub-conscious mind

- Tapping into our sub-conscious mind is the key to manifestation magic

The Manifestation Process

The actual process of Sigil Magick is quite simple and straight-forward as you'll soon discover as you read on. It can be useful to think of sigils and manifesting as an experiment. We can't be sure how and when our desires will manifest. Start with simple things to manifest to master the process. e.g.) simple material objects (a torch, a book, an item of clothing), an animal encounter or new music etc. You can go on to manifest more juicy things when you've mastered the basic process! Practicing manifesting a more abundant, magical universe definitely feels like a good thing to do…

Symbology And The Power Of Symbols

Symbology has been a part of humanity since we first began scratching images on cave walls. The first written languages were entirely symbolic. The evolution of the written word and the history of symbols are inseparably tied. As man's understanding grew so did his connection to symbols as the ideas they once linked to transformed into actual words. However, the influence of symbols never waned and they grew in historic cultures as mythic runes of power. Different cultures viewed symbols differently, each trying to define the distinct power as it pertained to their own beliefs.

The feeling of power from symbols is the oldest form of symbolism. You feel it when the moon, rising over water, fills you with romance, or a birds song brings a smile to your face. As we process sounds and sights, we cannot help tying the symbols to something more. These natural symbols first drove man to express himself in lasting depiction of his view of transpirations.

The spoken word may have evolved after the use of symbology by primitive man. The first cave drawings appear to tell stories. Some people believe this to be a literal telling of events, man using pictograms rather than simple grunts and gestures, in order to more accurately describe things such as military victory and great hunts. These symbols would allow for a single story to be told, instead of the distorted version that is usually passed with oral traditions incalculably exacerbated by primitive language. While this theory is popular with logophiles, some of the more spiritually inclined believe the depictions were used to invoke the mythic abilities of the people, creatures and events depicted.

The inexplicable power of symbols filled humans with both curiosity and wonder. From witchcraft, sorcery, and alchemy using symbols to alter the physical state of the world around them to different Christian sects battling over the weight of iconography, people are passionate about symbols. To this day, The Bible carries with it a feeling of personal connection with the divine it gained when it first empowered the masses. Some symbols and their purpose are simple like a Star of David or the Yin Yang. But whether you are identifying a bold black star and crescent as a muslim symbol or evaluating whether a swastika evokes feelings of happiness, regret, or sadness, the symbol is always greater than the words used to describe it. It is the embodiment of the ideas behind it. The waves of emotion that the symbol evokes is the very reason so much spirituality must be connected to the symbol. This is why, even to the nonreligious, the first rays of the sun can induce feelings of hope and well-being.

The mysterious, emotion invoking power of symbols move people today. Over hundreds of years the connotation has changed and symbols can take radical new roles in modern life. Recently PepsiCo spent about a million dollars to redesign their brand logo to a cleaner and more dynamic representation of planetary magnetics and the illustration of a smile. The transition may end up costing them hundreds of millions of rebranding in the long run. The R. J. Reynolds company shelled out a cool ten million to anti-youth smoking campaigns in response to outrage over its use of an anthropomorphic, slightly phallic, camel character. The way these symbols are instantly recognised and associated in our lives has proven to be a lucrative endeavour for both branding advisors and the corporate entities they represent. A type of casual shorthand begun, where sounds and symbols are now used in lieu of slogans. Now something seemingly clear cut like the written, *"Ho Ho Ho,"* may reference Santa Claus or The Green Giant, but people instantly recognise a solid green Christmas tree or Ronald McDonald. The transition has not diminished the power of words, sometimes the words themselves can be a symbol. The ability of a popular song riff may make your head bob and toe tap or remind you that your truck can carry you to a, *"great unknown."* Symbology has so permeated our lifestyle that it even affects the way we are connecting to each other.

With the dawn of smart phones and social media reaching their zenith in tandem, a new type of symbol has replaced the icon and logo as the most seen symbology in our everyday life, the emoji. Originally used primarily by teens of the late 90's to text, emoji have expanded to what can essentially be described as a new language. Symbols can be used to replace lines of text and placing whole ideas and concepts in a single character. This is beginning to expose a de-evolution of the effectiveness of symbols. Many are beginning to view the misunderstandings and multiple interpretations of these conversations as evidence of a breakdown in youth communication. The visibility of these blunders, with a natural resistance to change, may partially be to blame for the idea that there is a growing problem. It would be tremendously difficult to argue that this *de*-evolution of symbology hasn't filled a useful niche in a society of ease and convenience.

Another exposed, though not as recent, danger of symbology is the ease in which it can be used to mislead. This danger is one that may be more damaging than simple ill-ease with the older generations. Powerful symbols have been used in propaganda to manipulate the masses. This concept of using symbols is based on the emotions we already have tied to a symbol itself and associating that emotional response to a new concept or idea. The Nazi Party in Germany used ancient runes and bold colours to associate themselves with pure power. Sometimes the subversion is much more subtle, like an easily debunked claim that a certain politician was hanging muslim curtains. Media has taken to using harsh musical tones and black and white footage to invoke a subtle ominous feeling to things that don't necessarily worry viewers. Even hate groups have used religious symbols to inoculate themselves to deep scrutiny.

It is these innovations, traditions, dangers and wonders that add and illustrate the power of symbols in our lives. It may seem like history or trivial knowledge but if simple symbols can alter so much and make such an impact on society, maybe we should re-evaluate the importance in our personal lives. Sometimes your day should start with the hope and new beginning of a sunrise. Maybe you could use more bold colours to tap into your own passion as you face your day. Many people take comfort in wearing religious symbols and relics, dressing in their faith or touching the symbol in times of need. These symbols can be used to evoke new energy into your daily life in many new ways. Next time you have to re-evaluate a force for change in your life, you shouldn't underestimate the power of symbols.

What are Thought Forms?

The mind is an extremely powerful entity, and it gives us the conditioning and endurance required to get through some of the hardest possible times in life. With the right mentality and a strong, engaging mind you can greatly enhance your quality of life and consistency of success throughout life. However, just how powerful is the human mind? Can it really emit more power and strength than we see on a day-to-day basis?

For example, take the idea of *Thought Forms*. A Western occult tradition that has been built on the idea of the ancient Tulpa, this is a concept within mysticism that someone can create a being or an object purely through the power of their mental power and discipline. Any mind-made or unreal apparition/entity can be considered to be a Tulpa. As you can imagine, this is quite a significant thought process; *is it really possible to conjure things using the power of your mind?*

The actual *"thought form"* was first used in a 1927 translation of the Tibetan Book of the Dead, by John Reynolds. In a note inside the English translation of another book, covering the life of Garab Dorje, a Tulpa or *"thought form"* is described as *"an emanation of a manifestation."* In Western society, the idea of a Tulpa and the *"thought form"* is almost identical – however, the origins differ.

Whereas in Tibetan ideals the power of the Tulpa comes from mental and spiritual power and control, in Western society it's more related to the idea of magic or conjuring. It's believed by many to be the result of telegraphic mind processing, allowing our minds to actually put what we are thinking about in front of us directly – it may not be real, but it allows us to visualise and control our thoughts to emit full control.

The idea of thought forms can be quite frightening – the belief that we can create a new mind entirely is something that feels very much at odds with the stark realities of the world around us.

However, in a society built on ignoring the more spiritual side of the world – instead looking at things that are clearly here such as manmade products and consumerist ideals – it's no surprise that the idea of Tulpa or *"thought forms"* sounds like it belongs on our 50" TV screens rather than in the capable hands of everyone.

But we can and do create Thought Forms everyday! We do have the power to perform acts of manifestation like this through our incredible human consciousness. And with the simple methods in this guidebook, you'll be able to focus your intention, create a desirable Thought Form in the form of a Sigil, energise it, and send it forth into the Universe to work it's manifestation magic!

Chaos Magick

Chaos Magick is a term that holds prominence in many different walks of life – from famous fictional content such as Warhammer to popular occult movies throughout time; it's a large part of the "good" and "evil" sides of magick we all read about in popular media. However, the actual world of Chaos Magick goes far beyond a timeline in fictional worlds – it's a pragmatic series of beliefs that are built around magical traditions with a lot of influence from Eastern philosophies.

What we would refer to today as Chaos Magick, though, stems from somewhere a little closer to home – West Yorkshire, England. Ray Sherwin and Peter Carroll are deemed to be the progenitors of this school of magick, and it was in 1978 that they established the Illuminates of Thanateros (IOT). Alongside this and the Psychonaut book released in 1981 by Carroll, they stand as two of the genuine pillars of modern Chaos Magick. *(The main source of chaos magickal theory and practice actually goes back further though, into the early twentieth century, with an interesting fellow called, Austin Osman Spare; more about him coming up in the next chapter...)*

Based around the ideal that belief is merely a tool to help you get the results you want out of life, Chaos Magick is a hugely individualistic process. Seen by others to be troublesome individuals pent up on causing revolution and changing the world, the ideals of those who follow Chaos Magick are quite different to the usual school of thought. They draw heavily from the likes of Discordianism, as well as the growing publication and popularity of other forms of modern magick. It's a practice where they believe that everything they are using – the belief and ability of Gods, for example – is merely a psychology, and not something that is genuinely happening. In this way, they differ wholly from the traditional sense of a Magick practitioner.

Becoming a Sigil Magician

Meet Magick Man Austin Osman Spare

Many names across the history of the United Kingdom stand out for various reasons – some of them for the right reasons, others less so. For example, the name Austin Osman Spare is one which draws many controversial glances and incites debate even today. Born 30th December 1886, he was to become one of the prominent artists and, at the same time, occultists of his generation. He worked as both a draughtsman and a painter, and was known for his excellent designs of extremely adult imagery of both a violent and a sexual nature.

He was also a huge fan of occult techniques like automatic drawing and writing which were based on many different theories to do with the conscious mind. He was born into a family of working class parents in London, and worked his way through life with a keen interest in art. He trained as a draughtsman at the Royal College of Art in South Kensington, and it was at this time that he developed his own philosophical ideals on the occult.

He authored several grimoires such as Earth Inferno and The Focus of Life, further adding to his controversial character. He gained fame by being the youngest ever entrant at the 1904 Royal Academy summer exhibition.

Following his early fame, he went on to produce two art magazines known as Form and The Golden Hind, before he was conscripted into the First World War to work as a war artist. Following the war, he spent a large part of his life in poverty despite having varying degrees of success through his exhibitions.

The 1930s saw a revival in his work as surrealism took over the London art scene, reviving his fame slightly until the breakout of the Second World War. This led to him following back into obscurity until his death in 1956. His legacy was continued by a close friend by the name of Kenneth Grant, a Thelemite author.

He was revived as a purpose of public interest in the 1970s when his art again came to the fore, where many retrospective exhibits took place across London to honour his work. He has also been the case of several books over the years, with Phil Baker releasing a title about the artist in 2011.

A controversial figure due to his rather rigorous belief in the world of the occult, he played a significant part in helping the art scene in London move forward and develop beyond it's then rather close-minded style.

Most importantly for the purpose of this book, is that Spare developed the practicalities of Sigil Magick and the use of a concentrated trance state, which he referred to as *"the Gnostic state"* or *"Gnosis,"* to empower sigils. Most of the sigil work available reiterates Spare's technique, including the construction of a short sentence of intent, the reduction of the sentence, and the artistic recombination of the remaining letters to form the sigil.

Let's now uncover the practical secrets of Sigil Magick...

What Do You Want? (Step 1)

Think about something you desire or want. You can come up with anything for this, either material objects, wonderful experiences, learning experiences, or even spiritual experiences. You'll want to phrase it in a Positive Statement:

e.g.) *"I'll stop being poor"* ==> *"I will be inspired with a new money making idea."*

But let's start with something simple so you can learn the actual Sigil Magick process and get more familiar with it:

e.g.) *"I want to be given a new coat"*

The thing with the statement above is that it is stated as a desire. We want to reformulate the statement into a phrase that is more positive and expectant:

e.g.) *"I will be given a new coat"*

Using the phrase, *"I will,"* is the best way of starting your statement of intent. Here are a few more examples:

"I will make a new friend"

"I will discover amazing new music"

"I will obtain a new book that is really helpful to me"

Contrast Lists

Often times it's easier to think about what we don't want rather than clarify what we do want. This is where the concept of *Contrast Lists* comes in useful. You write down all the things you don't like in the *Contrast* column and then with each statement you ask yourself, **"So what do I want?"**, and then you write a *Positive Statement* of what you do want in the *Clarity* column. This can be an excellent way of clarifying what you do actually want and often speeds up the process considerably.

Contrast	Clarity
"I don't want to feel lonely"	"I will have more fun with friends"
"I don't want to feel bored"	"I will feel wonderfully inspired"
"I don't want to be single"	"I will be in a new loving relationship"

This method comes from Michael J Losier's, Clarity Through Contrast Worksheet from his Law of Attraction work.

So, grab a pen and piece of paper and come up with something simple to manifest for the purposes of learning the process and create a statement of intent starting with, *"I will..."*

Sentence Reduction (Step 2)

Using, *"I will discover amazing new music,"* as our statement of intent, let's now proceed with the second step; sentence reduction. To reduce our original statement we start off by removing all the vowels in the sentence; so that's the following letters; A, E, I, O, U. You can simply put a line through each vowel letter:

Ɨ will discover amazing new music

Next, put a line through all the duplicate letters remaining in the sentence:

I will discover amazing new music

So now the only remaining letters are as follows:

d v r z g

D V R Z G (*in capitol letters*)

Create A Symbol With The Remaining Letters (Step 3)

What we do now is create a graphical symbol by combining all the remaining letters. You can do this in whatever way feels best to you. It doesn't need to be a work of art, as you can tell from my example below. However if you are artistic it can be a really nice exercise to draw beautiful sigils; take a look at the wonderful sigils my artist friend, Yenna Wolf, created below my example:

My Simple Sigil Example: *"I will discover amazing new music"*

Artistic Sigil Examples:

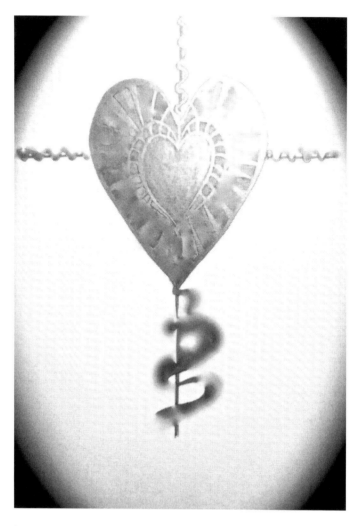

"I will discover wonderful new music"

The remaining letters after *Sentence Reduction*:

D V R Z G

"I will acquire an amazing new book"

The remaining letters after *Sentence Reduction*:

Q R M Z G B K

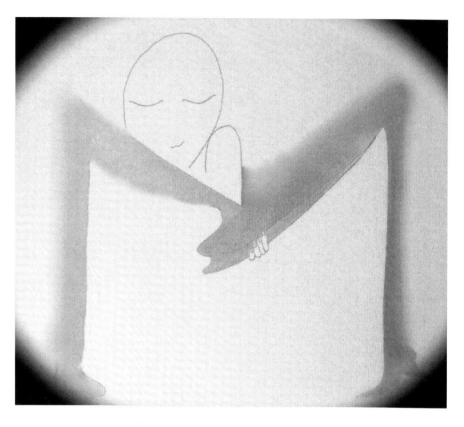

"I will make a new friend"

The remaining letters after *Sentence Reduction*:

M K F R D

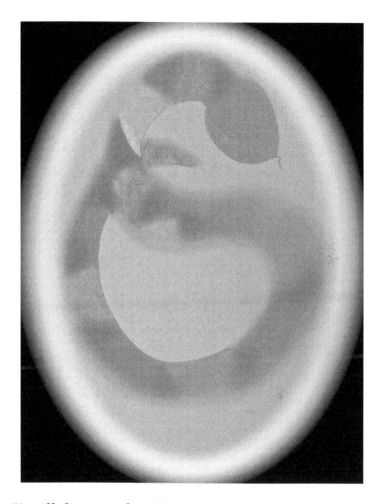

"I will discover love"

The remaining letters after *Sentence Reduction*:

W D S C R

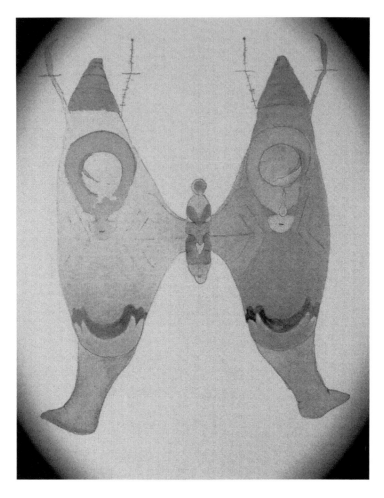

"I will have a profound spiritual experience"

The remaining letters after *Sentence Reduction*:

W H V F D S T X R C

"I will discover a new spiritual teacher"

The remaining letters after *Sentence Reduction*:

D V N P H

Energise and Activate the Sigil (Step 4)

Now your sigil is ready to be energised and activated. You can do this in a number of ways. Basically this is done by visualising your sigil in an altered state of consciousness and casting it forth into the Universe to manifest. This trance state, commonly known as *the Gnostic state*, can be fairly easily achieved with a little practice and is essential for achieving good results.

The Gnostic Trance State

The Gnostic state or Gnosis was a term coined by Chaos Magick author Peter Carroll. It's defined as an altered state of consciousness that is necessary for most magickal acts. This idea differs to older concepts of magical power which held energies, spirits or symbolic acts as the source of magical power. The Gnostic state is similar to the Buddhist *Samadhi* which was made popular in western esoteric circles by Aleister Crowley and Austin Osman Spare.

The state of Gnosis is achieved when your mind is single pointedly focussed on just one Thought Form. There are different ways of achieving this state of consciousness and one of the main benefits is that you can send the thought form directly into your subconscious mind, bypassing the *"psychic censor"* or critical ego-mind that has a tendency to sabotage one's efforts.

5 Ways to the State of Gnosis

1. Meditation

Basically with meditation you go into an altered state by focussing on your breathing, visualising or reciting mantras.

When you have reached a deep level of meditative equipoise you would visualise the sigil, make it brighter and brighter and then imagine sending it off into the universe; this only needs to be a second or two.

You then return to normal consciousness and quickly move on to Step 5: Forget About it! - Inducing Amnesia...

2. Exhaustion from Dancing

You can reach the state of Gnosis by dancing your socks off! Put your favourite music on LOUD and dance, dance, dance! When you feel exhausted, slump down into your favourite chair, focus on your breathing and then visualise your sigil clearly in your mind; make it big and bright and then intend it off into the Universe to manifest for you.

You then return to normal consciousness and quickly move on to Step 5: Forget About it! - Inducing Amnesia...

3. Hold an Uncomfortable Position for a Long Time

Another way to reach Gnosis is to put your body into an uncomfortable position for a long time. When the burn is getting really intense, visualise your sigil, make it big and bright in your mind's eye and then imagine sending it off into the Universe to manifest.

You then return to normal consciousness and quickly move on to Step 5: Forget About it! - Inducing Amnesia...

4. The Hypnagogic/Hypnopompic State

The state of consciousness you are in just before you fall asleep is known as the hypnagogic state. Your brainwaves have lowed down in this state and you can enter Gnosis easily from there. So ideally you would find yourself entering into the daydreamy hypnagogic state, visualise your sigil nice and bright, intend it into the Universe to manifest, and then fall asleep.

5. Orgasm

The traditional Sigil Magick method, which is actually easier and more fun than the other methods, is through the use of orgasm; either through self masturbation or sex with a partner. So this is actually a form of *Sex Magick*: *"Sex magic is any type of sexual activity used in magical, ritualistic or otherwise religious and spiritual pursuits. One practice of sex magic is using the energy of sexual arousal or orgasm with visualization of a desired result. A premise of sex magic is the concept that sexual energy is a potent force that can be harnessed to transcend one's normally perceived reality."* (wikipedia.org)

You start off by exciting yourself through whatever sexual method you prefer and then as you reach climax you visualise your sigil. Make it brighter and brighter and then imagine sending it off into the Universe; this only needs to last one or two seconds.

You then return to normal consciousness and quickly move on to Step 5: Forget About it! - Inducing Amnesia...

Note: For *double the fun* you could collaborate with your partner in sigil creation and then, while having sex, visualise and send forth the sigil during a shared orgasmic climax.

Visualisation Tip: Look at your sigil drawing a few times and then close your eyes and visualise it to help you remember it before you actually activate it. Remember you don't need to visualise it perfectly – just enough of the symbolic representation so your sub-conscious mind *gets it!*

Forget About it! - Inducing Amnesia (Step 5)

This step is really important because once we've sent the Thought Form (*the sigil*) into our subconscious mind (*which is connected to the greater Universe*), we need to forget about our statement of desire in order to stop our ego-mind from sabotaging our efforts with self doubt, self criticism, feelings of worthiness etc.

So the first thing to do when you've energised and activated your sigil (Step 4 above) is to banish your sigil drawing. You do this simply by ripping it up and throwing it in the bin. You could also burn it instead if you wish.

You now get busy with something else; do the washing up, go for a walk, start reading an interesting book, watch a video, ring someone up etc. This is important because it helps to take your mind off the original intent and re-focus your mind on to other things.

Sigil Making Tip: Create a few sigils in one session and then put them in a drawer. You can then pick one at random in a few days time to energise and activate it. Doing this will help you forget what each sigil symbolises. This is the ideal situation because it means the whole process has become sub-conscious; *right where we want it to be.*

Sigil Magick Step-by-Step Summary

What Do You Want? (Step 1)

Come up with something you want to manifest. Grab a piece of paper and write your statement of intent at the top starting with the phrase, *"I will..."*, remembering to keep the statement positively framed.

> e.g.) "I will make a new friend"

> e.g.) "I will discover amazing new music"

> e.g.) "I will be inspired with a new money making idea"

Sentence Reduction (Step 2)

Start off by removing all the vowels from your original statement of intent in Step 1.

e.g.) *"I will discover amazing new music"*

I will discover amazing new music

Now remove all the duplicate letters remaining in the sentence:

I will discover amazing new music

So now the only remaining letters are as follows:

d v r z g

D V R Z G (*in capitol letters*)

Create A Symbol With The Remaining Letters (Step 3)

You now combine the remaining letters above into a symbol; which becomes the sigil. You can do this in whatever way feels best for you. Just keep it simple so it will be easy to visualise; look at my example below:

Energise and Activate the Sigil (Step 4)

Basically you need to go into a trance state (Gnosis) and then visualise your sigil and imagine sending it off into the Universe to manifest for you. Getting into the gnostic state is most easily achieved through orgasm.

Forget About it! - Inducing Amnesia (Step 5)

This step is important because it helps stop the ego-mind from sabotaging our efforts. Once you've energised and activated your sigil (Step 4), rip up your sigil drawing and throw it in the bin.

And then get busy with something else to occupy your conscious ego-mind; do the washing up, go for a walk, start reading an interesting book, watch a video, ring someone up etc.

Spiritual Sigils

You can use Sigil Magick to manifest all your material desires but it can be much more interesting to manifest spiritual experiences. Maybe you want to manifest a profound spiritual learning experience or maybe you want to manifest more love and peace in your life. Or you could experiment with using Sigil Magick to manifest changes in your family or community; e.g.) *"I will experience more harmonious relationships in my community"* or *"I will experience more love in my family."*

To give you an example from my own life, I was living in the Findhorn eco-village in northern Scotland, and decided to experiment with the following sigil:

"I will have a profound spiritual experience."

Five days later I was helping out in the community kitchen and as a *thank-you* I was given a session ticket to attend a seminar given by well known spiritual teacher, Caroline Myss.

Now to be honest I had been very sceptical of Myss, mainly because I had experienced a few of her sycophantic fans following her every word in awe. So I went and sat in the back of the auditorium, feeling disinterested.

But was I in for a shock! After about an hour of her just rambling on, I was hit with a shift in attention. It felt as if she was focussing in on me. She was talking about confronting our own shadow aspects and how keeping them hidden is unhealthy and destructive. Basically my perception of it all was that I was being hit with a *Zen Stick* to acknowledge certain aspects of my shadow and share it with others. It was quite a wake up call.

This was quite an uncomfortable experience but it was imbued with truth. Fortunately the discomfort didn't last too long. Shortly after she launched into an amazing Bodhisattva style speech; it was a very moving talk about no matter how dark and depraved this world gets, she would never give up on increasing the amount of love in the world. It was very inspiring and brought tears to my eyes. But most importantly it reminded me, very poignantly, of why I started writing personal development books in the first place; the original intention of which I had forgotten due to the pressures of making a living. It was really powerful and inspired me into action; completing this book was a part of that process. My intention is to inspire people to access more of their human potential and in particular the power of the mind.

So, think about your own spiritual interests and come up with a *spiritual statement of intent*, make it into a sigil, and see what results you get; you never know, you may well have a very profound experience!

Here are some ideas to help get your started:

"I will meet a new spiritual teacher"

"I will have a wonderful new spiritual insight"

"I will experience an incredible level of peaceful bliss"

"I will be connected to universal love"

"I will experience a more harmonious community"

Sigil Magick Frequently Asked Questions (F.A.Q.)

Q. What is Magick?

It was infamous English Occult practitioner, Aleister Crowley, that added the 'K' onto the word *magic* to differentiate it from false stage magic. His definition of Magick was, *"the Science and Art of causing Change to occur in conformity with Will."*

Modern occult practitioner and Chaos Magick author, Peter J Carroll, says, *"Practicing magick merely involves bending, however slightly, the laws of probability. Every turning point in life hinges on the least alteration in the law of probability."*

So basically it's a way of tapping into your own mind power to help you manifest what you want in life.

Q. What is a Thought Symbol or Sigil?

Thought Symbols or Sigils are a Magickal method of transforming your desires and intentions into a visual symbol which you can energise and send into the universe to manifest for you. Please read the first chapter of this book to get a more in-depth explanation of Thought Symbols / Sigils.

Q. Do sigils really work?

As mentioned above in the Peter J Carroll quote, Sigil Magick, engages the power of the mind (*intention*) to bend the laws of probability in one's favour. You need to experiment with Sigil Magick and test the method out in your own experience. It's to be practiced, not theorised about, for achieving results in the real-world.

When you've been practicing Sigil Magick for a while you'll begin to become aware of things that have manifested from your efforts as it happens. e.g.) You'll obtain a jacket from a friend and instantly realise it's a manifested result from your Sigil Magick.

More interestingly, you'll become aware of *sigil success* a while after the manifestation has occurred; *in hindsight* in other words. An example from my own life was that I created a sigil to manifest, *"A fascinating rare book."* Now several weeks passed by and nothing had appeared. I thought, *"O well,"* and forgot about it. However I only realised a week or two later that this sigil had actually manifested what I wanted: Ingo Swann's book, *"Psychic Sexuality"* had been out of print for several years with second hand copies going for £170! It got released as a Kindle eBook about five weeks after I did the sigil.

Q. Is this witchcraft or black magic?

"Witchcraft" has been practiced for centuries and has a long history of both white magick (*doing good things for yourself and others*) and black magick (*sorely selfish intentions that can include harming others*). Practicing Sigil Magick is about clarifying your own desires and intentions and then manifesting them into your life. So it's really down to you if you practice black or white magic. *But you're a good person aren't you?* So do good things and make the world a better place!

Q. Can you still work towards manifesting the desire while the Sigil is in action?

You don't have to. It depends on what your outcome is. For instance if you intended to *"win the lottery,"* it would probably help *"bend the laws of probability"* in your favour if you went and bought some lottery tickets!

And as another example, if you intended to meet an inspiring new person, it would help you manifest that outcome by, of course, being pro-actively sociable.

More Sigil Magick Fun

There's a lot more you can do with Sigils other than the traditional *sentence reduction into visual symbol* method; which is the most appropriate process if you want to manifest specific material objects, persons, situations or experiences. The other sigil methods that follow are more catered for manifesting desired states of consciousness within yourself such as; *confidence, inspiration, humour, compassion and power etc.*

Magical Thought Symbol Cards

This method enables you to *program your sub-conscious mind* in a way that will enable you to experience more desirable states of mind in the future, automatically; basically the process creates unconscious triggers that will activate in the future spontaneously, giving rise to your chosen state of mind.

You start off in the traditional Sigil Magick way by creating your *statement of intent*. To get the best results you will want to chose a state of mind, energy or emotion that you'd like to experience more of; e.g.) *Fun, Joy, Laughter, Inspiration, Love, Enthusiasm* etc. Here are the Step-by-Step instructions for this method:

1. Create your *statement of intent* for the desired state you want to experience more of in the future. e.g.) *"I will experience more joy and laughter."*

2. Perform the standard Sigil Magick process described earlier in the *Sigil Magick Step by Step* chapter... (So when you've done, you will have a visual sigil drawn on paper.)

3. Look at your drawn sigil a few times so you can remember it's basic form. And then visualise your sigil as if it is a card in your hands; allow yourself to imagine duplicating that *sigil card* hundreds of times so it's like a large deck of cards in your hands.

4. Now pretend to physically grab hold of the deck and throw them high into the air and watch them land in random places all around you 360 degrees all the way off into the horizon.

NOTE: You can use your breath to imagine blowing the cards off in all directions to add another fun dimension to the ritual.

Thought Symbol Reminders

One of the other cool things you can do with sigils drawn on paper is use them as sub-conscious triggers. Again this specific method is best used for manifesting desired states of consciousness within yourself. For example you may want to experience more *light-heartedness.* So you would start off using the traditional Sigil Magick process by defining your *statement of intent*; e.g.) *"I will feel more light-hearted."* You would then, of course, reduce the sentence down and then transform the remaining letters into a sigil.

You can then use this sigil or thought symbol drawing to trigger your desired state of consciousness automatically. This is very simple to do; you just leave your sigil artwork lying around in random places. e.g.) Inside the bathroom cabinet, in the car glove box etc. You could hide it in drawers, books, under the pillow, in the garden shed and so on... Be sure to keep moving the sigil to different places so your desired state of consciousness gets triggered in different contexts, helping to generalise the effect.

Living the Magickal Lifestyle

Often times many of us focus on what we *don't* want in life; *we don't want to be poor* for example. *We don't want to be single* and so on... Practicing Sigil Magick helps to re-orientate your mind to **what you want**, rather than what you don't want!

Knowing what we want is usually a good first step. Part of the process of living in a Magickal world, *where we feel empowered to be able to manifest what we want in life*, is having the ability to be able to clearly define our desires, goals and intentions.

As you practice getting clear on what you want, creating and energising sigils, and experiencing results, you will increase your level of expectancy of success; *this is a great feeling!*

It's a really good exercise to brainstorm what you want in life. Grab a pen and paper and begin to jot down your desires, intentions, wishes and goals. Ask yourself questions such as:

1. *"What do I really want to manifest into my life?"*

2. *"What do I want more of?"*

3. *"What would be really cool?!"*

4. *"What would be a great goal to achieve this week/month/year?"*

5. *"What do I really value in life and what do I need in my life to experience more of that?"*

The next step is to pick one of those intentions and create a sigil. Doing so regularly will help you create a good habit. Write a few *statements of intention* in one session. Create a sigil everyday. Energise and activate one of your sigils. Get into the good habit of clarifying what you want in life, and get the Universe on your side to help you attain those outcomes with the practice of Sigil Magick.

Developing the *Magickal Mind-Set* will provide you with many benefits:

- You will become better at clarifying what you want in life.

- You'll get to know yourself better.

- You'll develop a more optimistic outlook on life.

- You'll look out for and actually start to perceive more opportunities that can enrich your life.

- Life will become more magical!

~ Happy Sigil-ing! ~

Further Reading

Thought Symbols: A Simple, Easy to Learn Process Which Will Bring All of Your Hopes, Dreams and Desires into Reality... Now - Edgar Maynard

Create a Servitor: Harness the Power of Thought Forms - John Kreiter

Practical Sigil Magic: Creating Personal Symbols for Success - Frater U.D.

Wealth Magick: The Secrets of Extreme Prosperity - Damon Brand

Other Books of Interest

The Book of Pleasure - Osman Austin Spare

Liber Null - Peter J. Carroll

Pop Magick - Grant Morrison

Made in the USA
Las Vegas, NV
01 April 2021

20586904R00024